Solar System Explorers

Mercury

Written by
Charis Mather

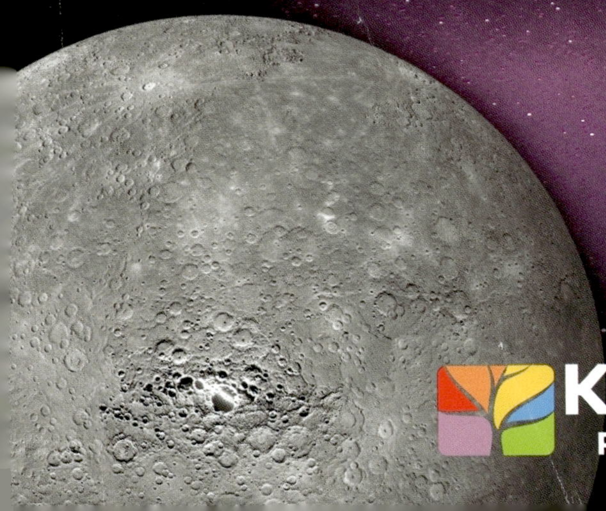

KidHaven
PUBLISHING

Published in 2026 by
KidHaven Publishing, an Imprint of
Greenhaven Publishing, LLC
2544 Clinton St., Buffalo, NY 14224

Written by: Charis Mather
Edited by: Noah Leatherland
Designed by: Amelia Harris

Cataloging-in-Publication Data
Names: Mather, Charis.
Title: Mercury / Charis Mather.
Description: Buffalo, NY : Kidhaven Publishing, 2026. | Series: Solar System Explorers | Includes glossary and index
Identifiers: ISBN 9781534549821 (pbk) | ISBN 9781534549838 (library bound) | ISBN 9781534549845 (ebook)
Subjects: LCSH: Mercury (Planet)—Juvenile Literature
Classification: LCC QB611 M38 2026 | DDC 523.41--dc25

Manufactured in the United States of America

CPSIA compliance information: Batch #CSKH26
For further information contact Greenhaven Publishing LLC at 1-844-317-7404.

Please visit our website, www.greenhavenpublishing.com.
For a free color catalog of all our high-quality books, call toll free 1-844-317-7404 or fax 1-844-317-7405.

Find us on

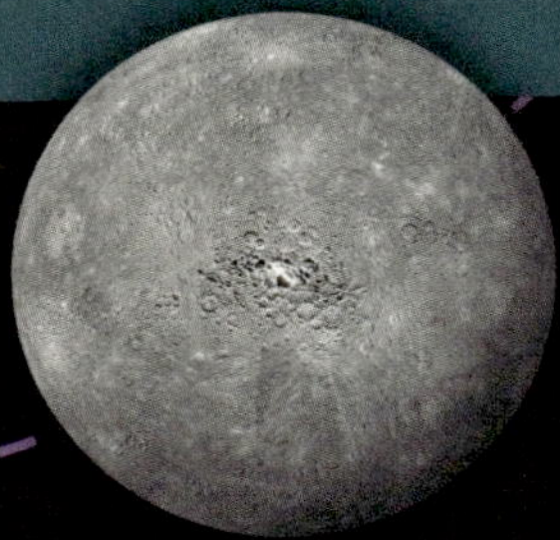

Image Credits

Images are courtesy of Shutterstock.com. With thanks to Getty Images, Thinkstock Photo and iStockphoto. Cover – 19 STUDIO, AspctStyle, andreysharonov, leshiy985. Recurring Images – thomas eder, YummyBuum, Sabelskaya. 4–5 – Sebastian Kaulitzki, 24K-Production. 6–7 – bilgeari, Dotted Yeti. 8–9 – buradaki, Sebastian Kaulitzki. 10–11 – AspctStyle. 12–13 – Daniil Disa, Vadim Sadovski. 14–15 – HelenField, BlueBackIMAGE, Pzykodegoat. 16–17 – Pzykodegoat, NASA/ Johns Hopkins University Applied Physics Laboratory/ Carnegie Institution of Washington, CC BY 2.0 <https://creativecommons.org/licenses/by/2.0>, via Wikimedia Commons. 18–19 – Perfect_kebab, 24K-Production, NASA, Public domain, via Wikimedia Commons. 20–21 – Marcel Drechsler, NASA, Public domain, via Wikimedia Commons. 22–23 – buradaki, NASA, Public domain, via Wikimedia Commons.

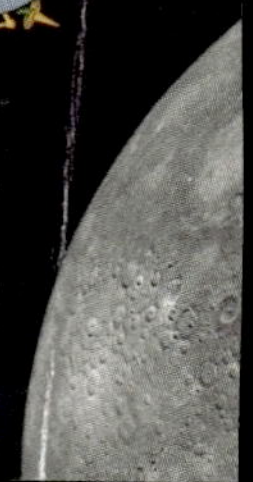

Contents

Words that look like this can be found in the glossary on page 24.

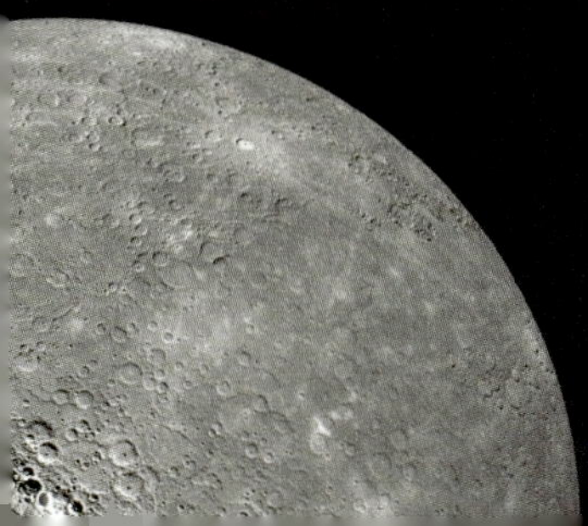

Let's Explore!

Are you ready to explore the solar system with us? The solar system is huge, but do not worry. We have a speedy spaceship to take us wherever we want to go.

The solar system has eight planets, five dwarf planets and hundreds of moons.

One by one, we are visiting all the planets in the solar system. There are so many interesting things to learn about each of these massive objects **orbiting** the sun.

Where Is Mercury?

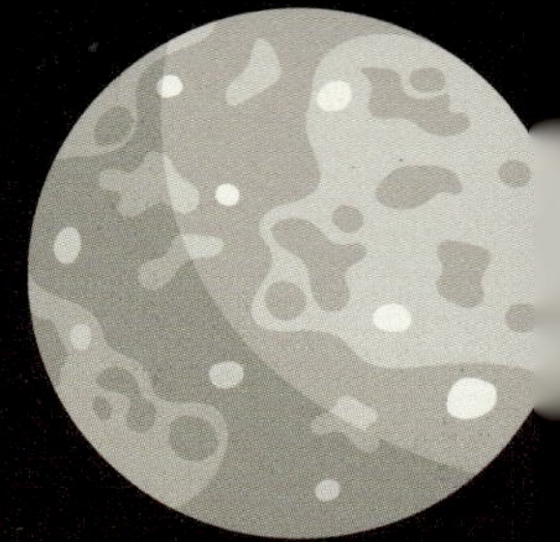

The planets in the solar system are constantly moving around the sun at different speeds and at different distances. If all eight were lined up, this would be their order:

Mercury is about 36 million miles (58 million km) away from the sun, which makes it the closest of the eight planets. The planet that comes closest to Mercury is Venus.

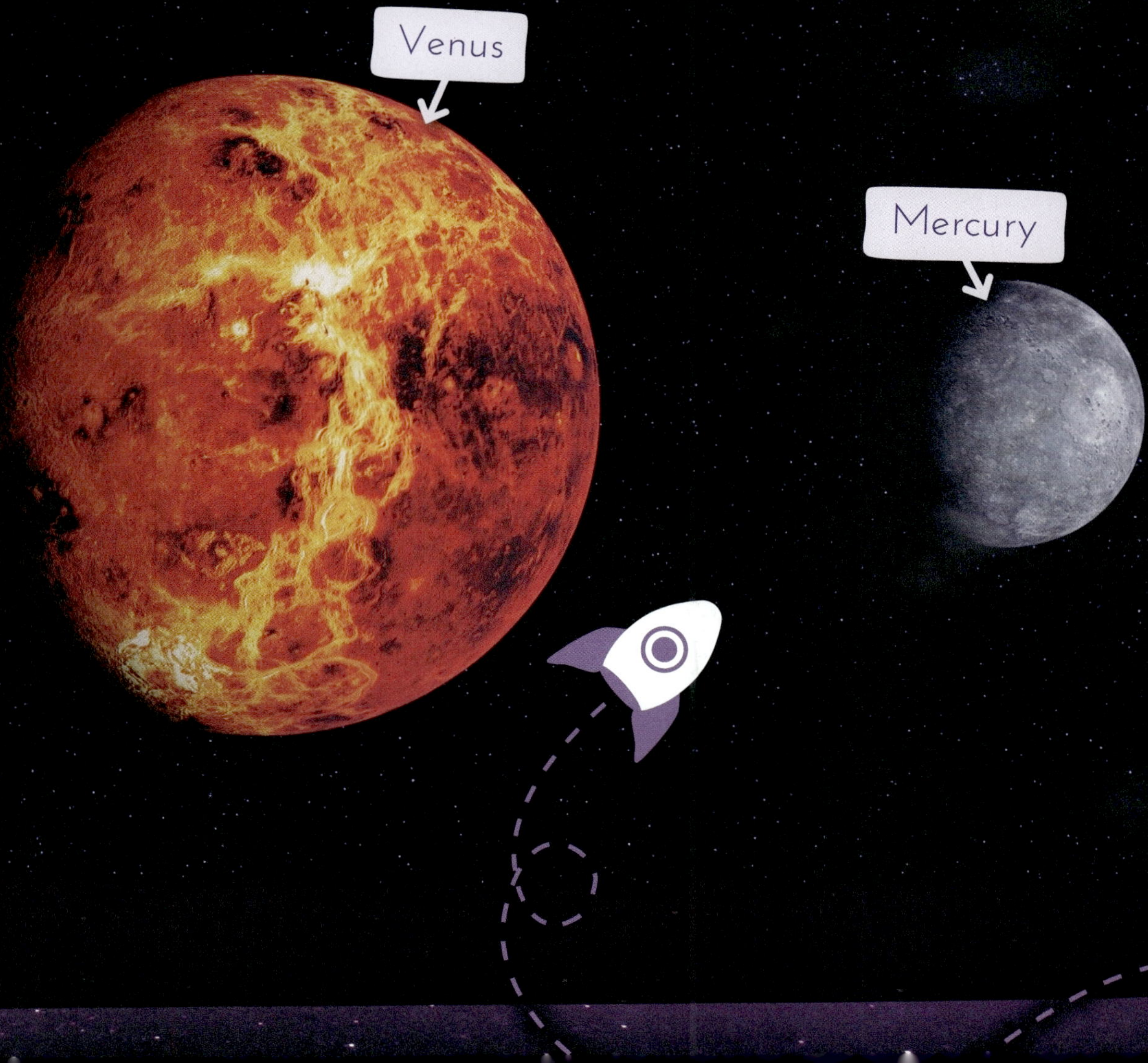

Round and Round

A year is the amount of time it takes a planet to orbit the sun. For Earth, a year takes 365 days. For Mercury, a year only takes 88 days.

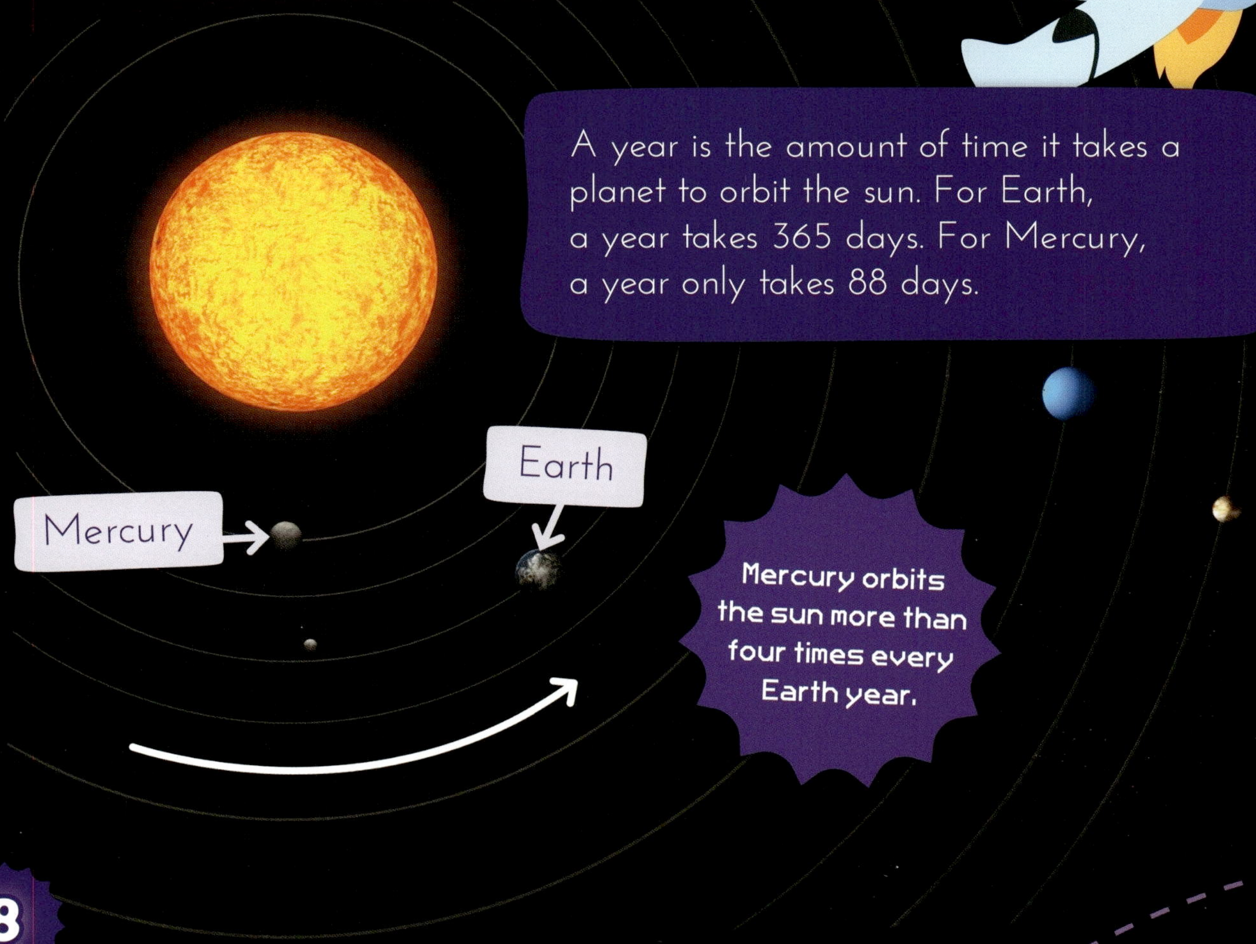

Mercury orbits the sun more than four times every Earth year.

Every planet spins as it orbits. One full spin is one day. On Earth, a day takes 24 hours. On Mercury, a day takes 1,408 hours. That is 59 Earth days.

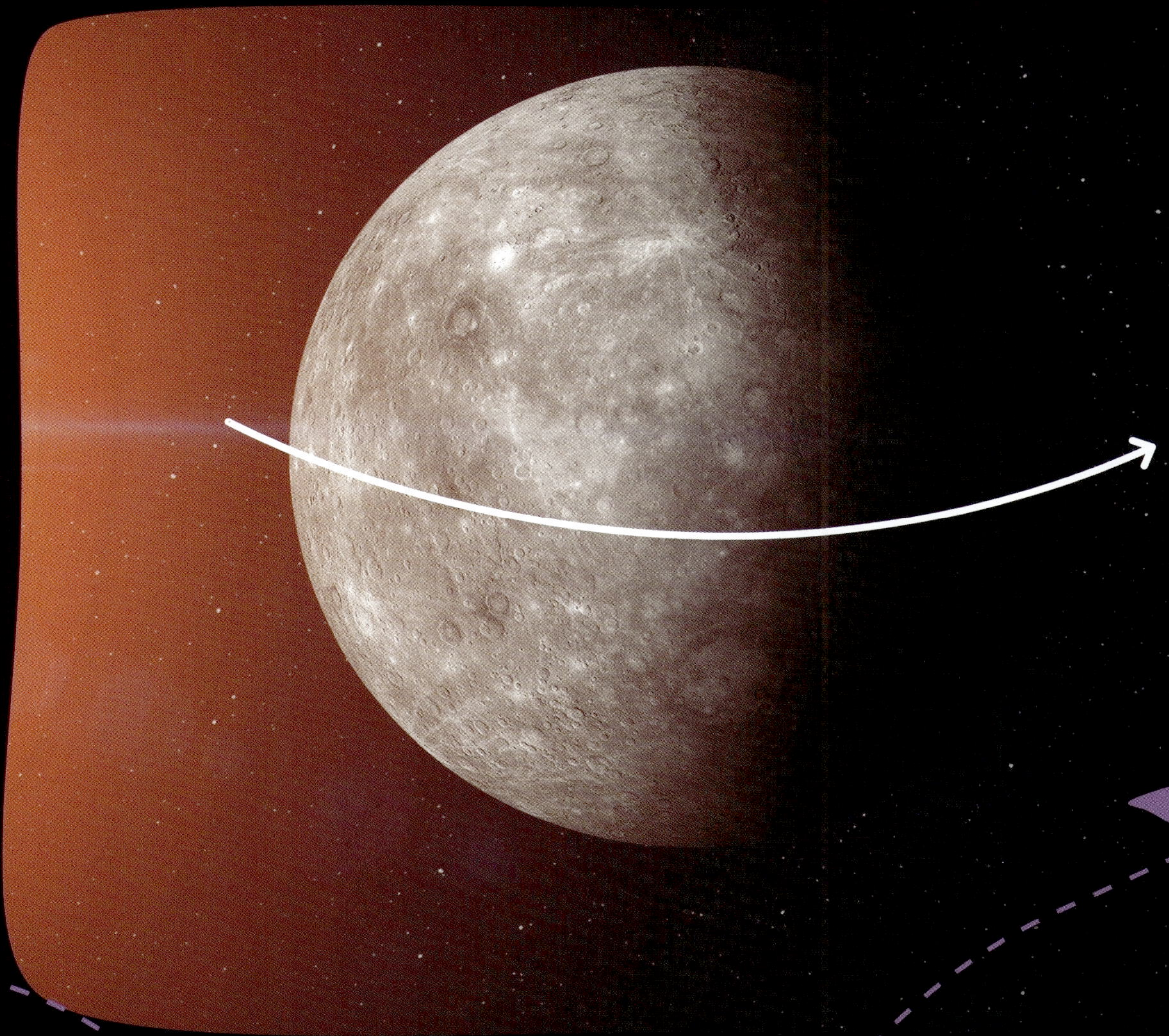

Planet Profile

Let's check the database for information about Mercury.

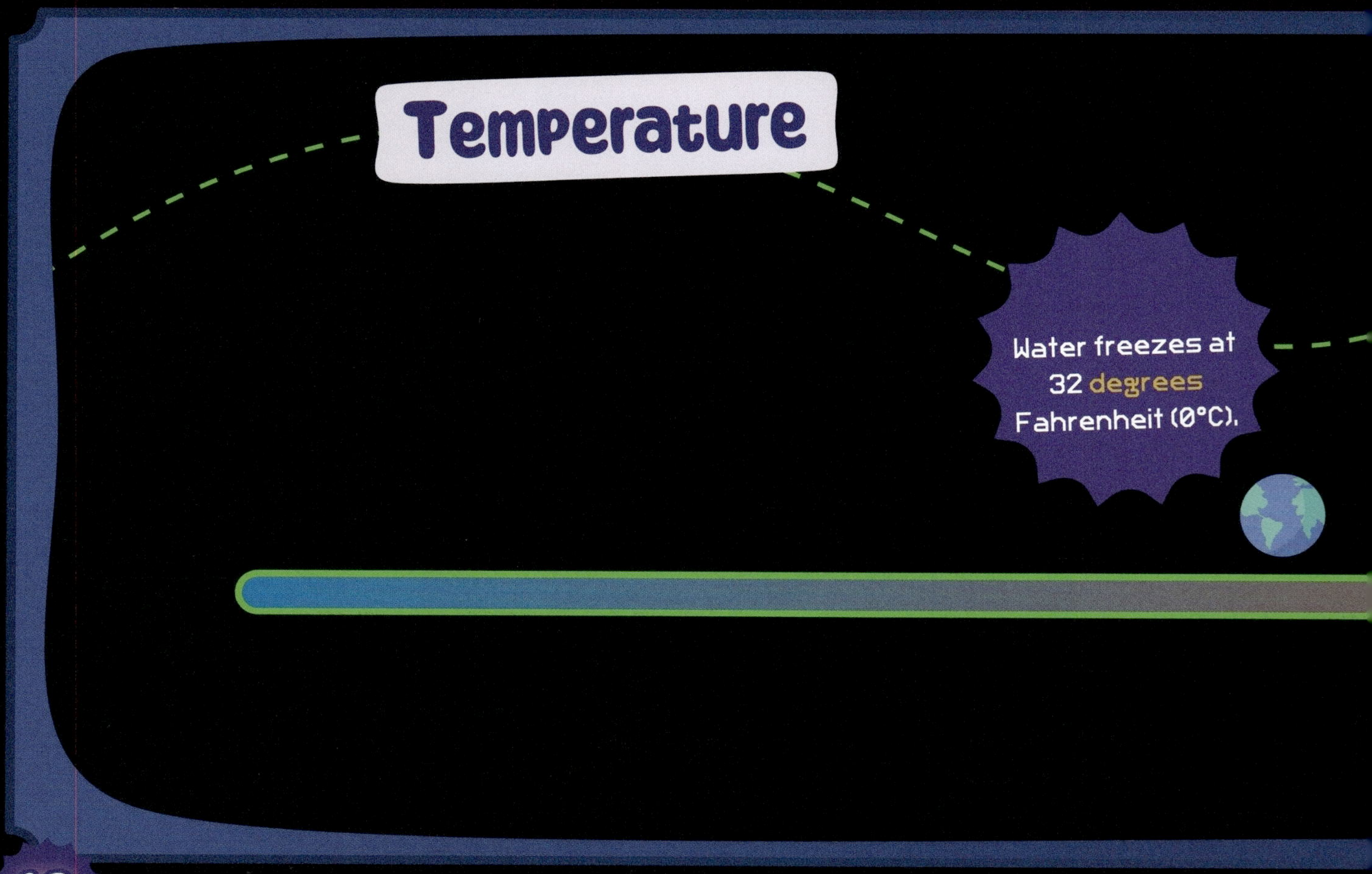

Size

- Around: 9,525 miles (15,329 km)
- Across: 3,032 miles (4,880 km)

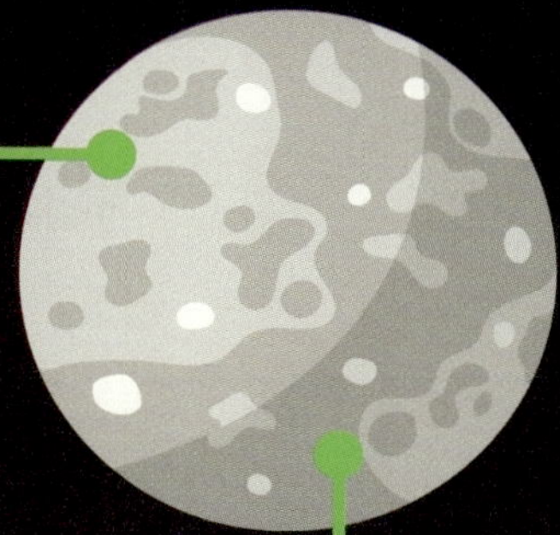

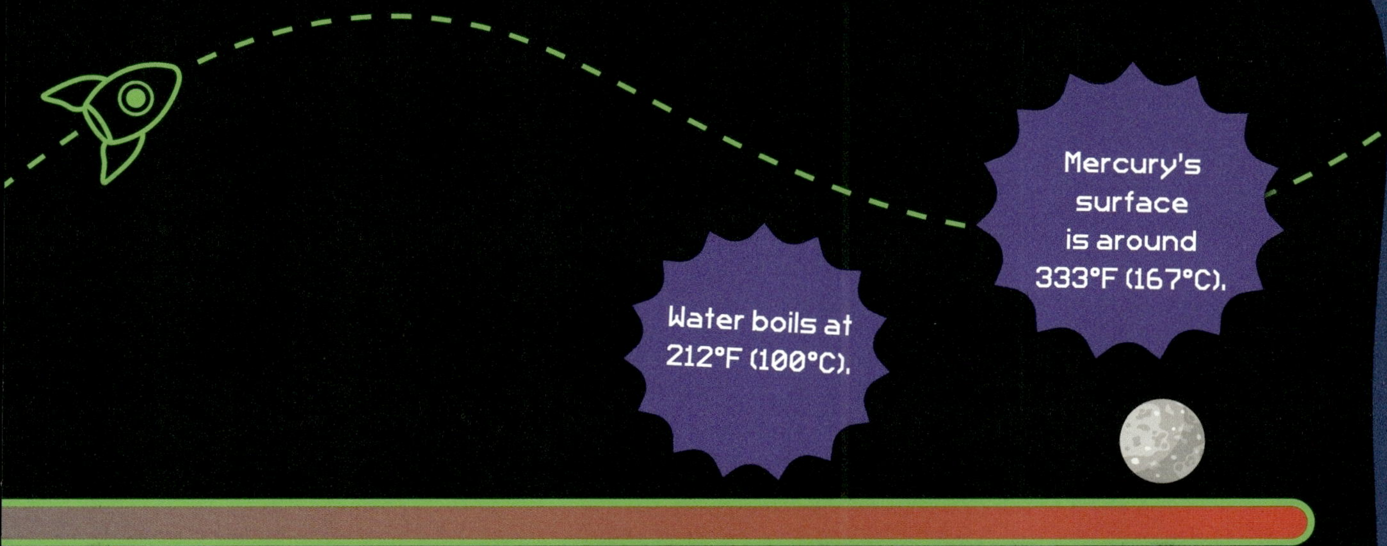

What Is Mercury Made Of?

Mercury is one of the solar system's four rocky planets. On the outside, Mercury looks a lot like Earth's moon. Its outer layer is covered in rock and dust.

Another word for a rocky planet is a terrestrial planet.

On the inside, Mercury has more layers.

Mantle

The mantle layer is made of hot, rocky material.

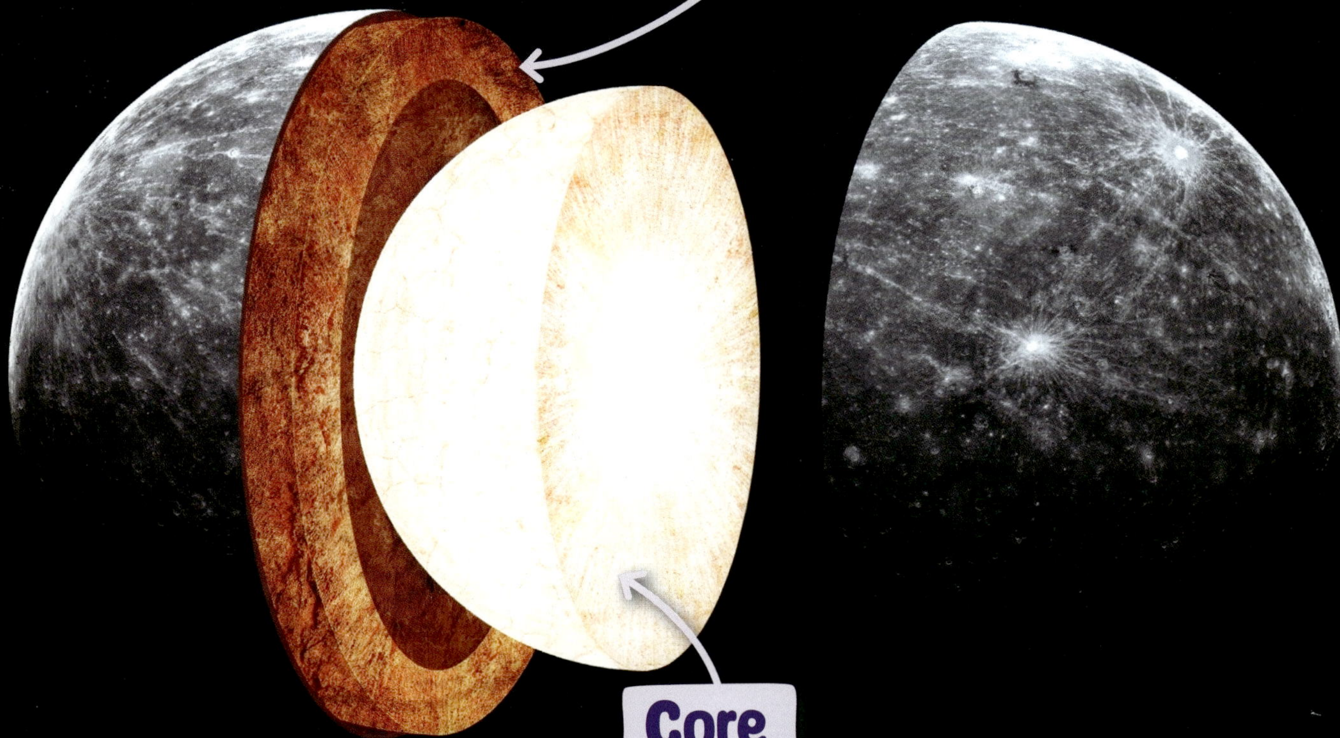

Core

Under the mantle is the core layer. The core is full of extremely hot iron, some of it **molten**.

Watching the Weather

Unlike Earth, Mercury does not have a **permanent** outer layer of **gas**. The sun blasts away most of Mercury's gases. All that is left is a very thin layer, called an exosphere.

Earth has a permanent layer of gas, called an atmosphere.

Mercury has a thin exosphere.

If we were standing on Mercury in our special suits, the sky would look black, even during the day. There would not be any clouds, rain, or any kind of weather except sunshine.

Is There Life on Mercury?

Without a proper atmosphere, Mercury is not habitable.

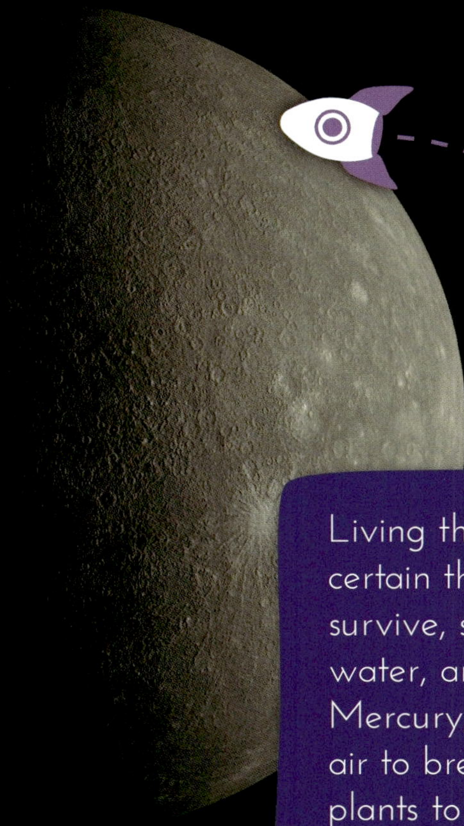

Habitable means that living things could **survive** there.

Living things need certain things to survive, such as air, water, and food. On Mercury, there is no air to breathe or for plants to use.

There may be some water on Mercury, but it is probably ice. Even though Mercury is close to the sun, some parts stay freezing cold, such as the shadowed areas in some **craters**.

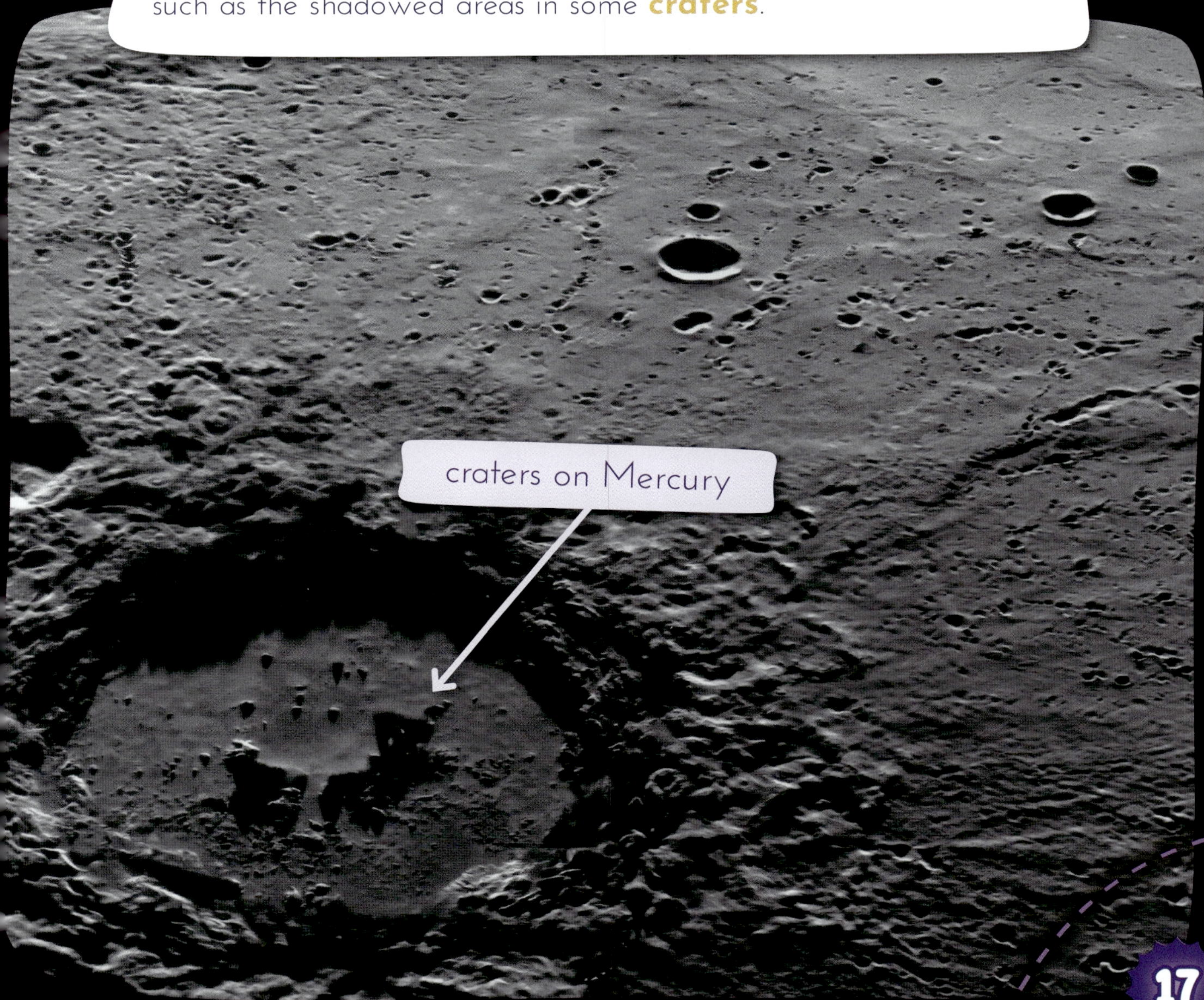

Covered in Craters

Even though Mercury is the smallest planet in the solar system, it has the most craters. Since Mercury does not have a thick atmosphere, there is nothing to stop **meteoroids** hitting it.

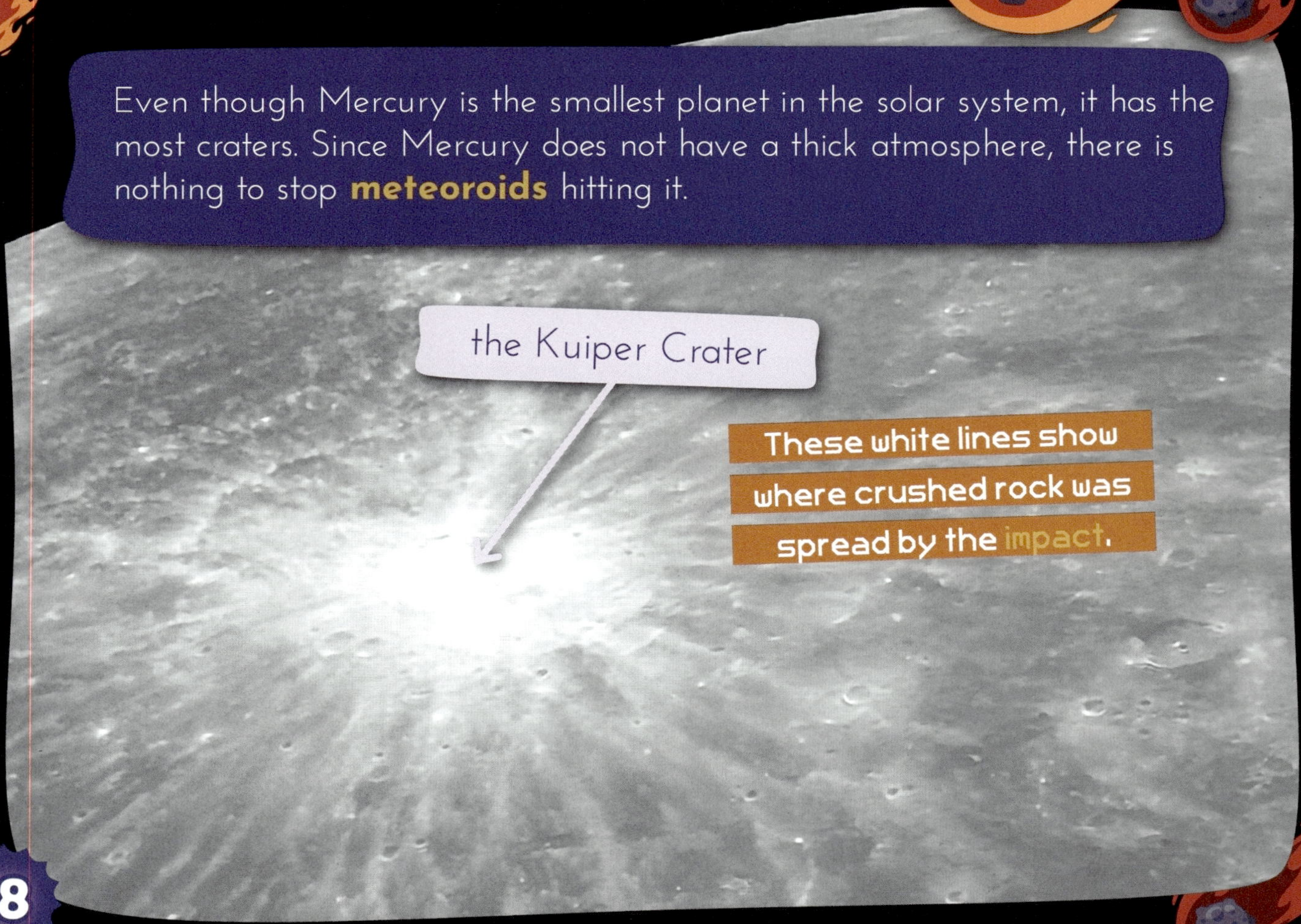

Craters that are larger than 185 miles (300 km) across are called basins. The Caloris Basin is more than 950 miles (1,525 km) across. It is so big that it contains many smaller craters inside it.

Spot the Satellites

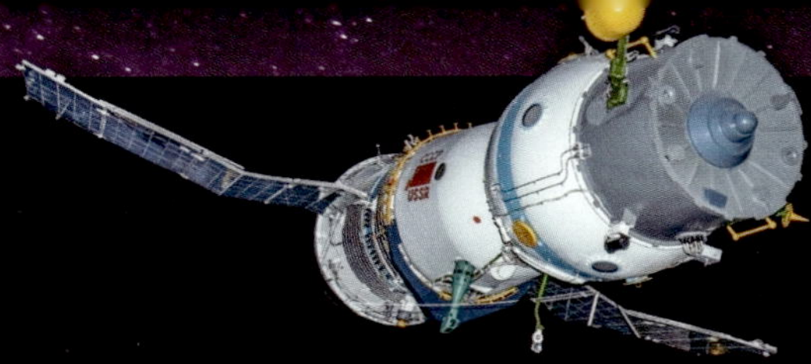

Most planets in the solar system have moons. However, Mercury does not. Mercury has much weaker **gravity** than the sun. This means that nearby objects get pulled toward the sun instead of into Mercury's orbit.

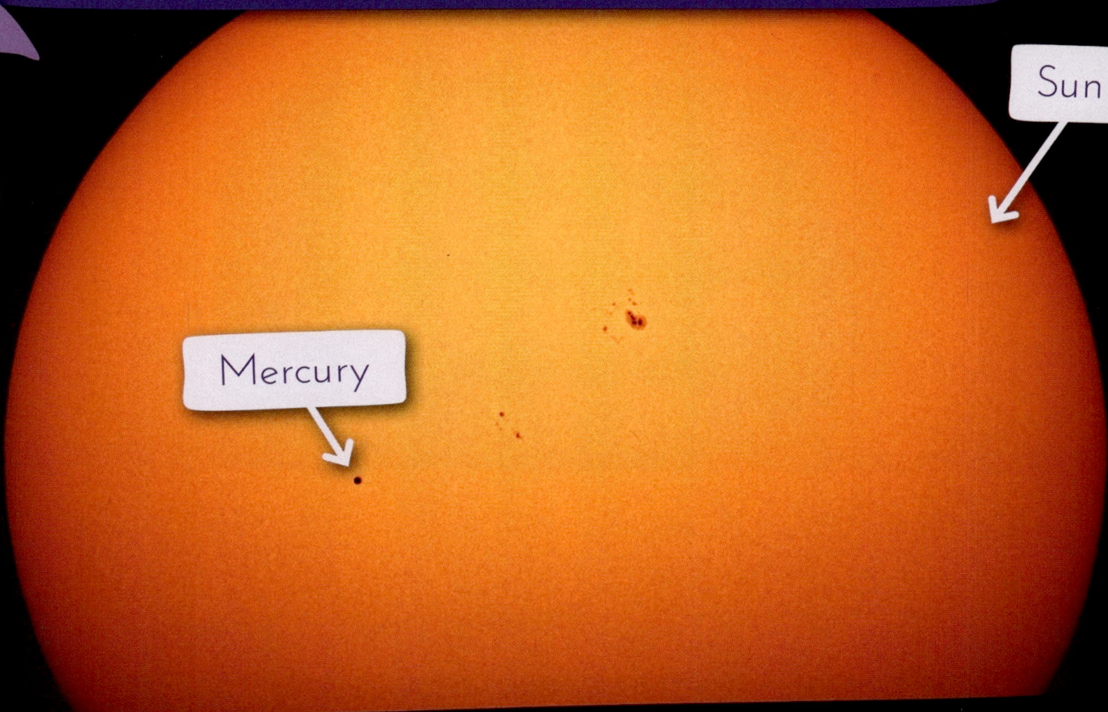

While Mercury does not have any moons of its own, it has had a human-made satellite called MESSENGER.

Satellites are objects that orbit other objects in space.

This satellite orbited Mercury for four years to help scientists understand more about the planet.

More to Explore

So, what do you think about Mercury, the solar system's smallest planet? Did you learn anything surprising? Finding out new things about space is one of our favorite things about being solar system explorers.

It is time to leave Mercury and visit a new planet. Are you ready for more adventures? There are plenty of stops waiting for us on our mission around the solar system!

Glossary

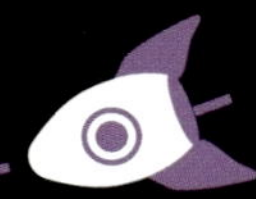

craters	large, shallow holes on the surface of something
degrees	measuring units used to explain how hot or cold something is
gas	a thing that is like air, which fills any space available
gravity	the force that pulls everything downward toward the center of large objects in space
impact	the act or force of one thing hitting another
meteoroids	small, rocky objects in space that move around the solar system
molten	turned to liquid because of heat
orbiting	moving around a star or planet in a curved path
permanent	lasting forever
survive	to stay alive

Index